SONS
OF
GLORY

KALEL PRATICO

ISBN: 978-1985755161

Copyright © 2018 by Kalel Pratico

TABLE OF CONTENTS

INTRODUCTION

Come on a journey with me through the scriptures to discover a blueprint for revival and the restoration of all things. The main passages I will be using are from Paul's third missionary journey and second visit to Ephesus. This is outlined in Acts 19 and 20.

The revival Paul experienced in Ephesus is one of the greatest recorded revivals in all of history. I will use this passage to show how God is going to move on a massive scale at the end of the age.

The other passages I will draw from are First and Second Corinthians along with the book of Ephesians. The epistles written to the Church at Corinth shed light on what was happening with Paul in the revival. They are relevant because Paul wrote them during and briefly after his second time in Ephesus when the revival happened. The book of Ephesians was written to the Church of Ephesus during Paul's first imprisonment in Rome. This epistle reveals the inner workings of what took place with Paul in the revival. Paul received understanding of how to carry revival into regions through healthy spiritual warfare while in Ephesus. He shares this information with the Ephesian Church.

The primary Bible translation I will use is the New American Standard Bible. If I am using the NASB, you will see no reference to the translation only book and verse. When using other translations, you will see an abbreviated reference of the translation being used.

Throughout the book I use the phrases, "sons of glory" and "glory carriers" interchangeably. These phrases are both descriptive of the same group of people God is raising up at the end of the age. The phrase "son" includes women as well. Men are the Bride of Christ and women are Sons of God. This title speaks about a position of relationship rather than a gender identity.

I encourage you that as you read this book, begin to ask Holy Spirit to give you understanding on what you are reading. My heart is that you won't only receive revelation but also encounter the One who desires experiential relationship with you.

There will be many sons who manifest the very nature and presence of the Holy One causing the created order to respond. Join me in discovering your identity as a son of glory.

Part One:
IDENTITY

Chapter One

KNOWLEDGE OF THE GLORY

For the earth will be filled with the knowledge of the glory of the

LORD as the waters cover the sea.

Habakkuk 2:14, ESV

Before the end of the age there will be a people who not only speak of the glory but carry it into all the earth. This manifestation of glory will begin the process of the restoration of all things. One of the most popular passages describing the end of the age is Mark 16:15, in which Jesus explains that in order for the end to come the Gospel must be preached to all creation.

When the Gospel is preached to all creation, it is another way of saying that the knowledge of the glory will cover the earth as the waters cover the sea. Who are the people who will carry the glory to all creation? The answer: you!

If you are a part of the body of Christ, you are a son of glory. As the end of the age approaches two dynamics will happen concurrently: God's plan, which is the restoration of all things, and the Devil's plan, which is the destruction of all things. Some people will be influenced by the enemy, and some will be influenced by God. My emphasis in this book will be on the restoration of all things and how that's connected to glory carriers.

An important distinction to make regarding the restoration of all things is that it doesn't just happen by accident. The restoration of all things happens as creation itself responds to sons. "The creation itself will be set free from its bondage to corruption and obtain the freedom of the glory of the children of God" (Romans 8:21).

The word "glory" in the Hebrew language is *Kabod*. This word is simply interpreted as the weighty presence of God. The Israelites saw this *Kabod* as a fire. "And to the eyes of the sons of Israel the appearance of the glory of the Lord was like a consuming fire on the mountain top" (Exodus 24:17). We will talk more about the glory of God and the various ways it manifests throughout this book. Glory carriers will bring the manifestation of God's fiery presence throughout all of creation to the point that it will cover the earth as the waters cover the sea.

To get a better picture of what the Lord is going to do through the coming glory, I am going to give you an example of what a glory carrier looks like.

Chapter Two

PAUL THE APOSTLE

For a wide door for effective work has opened to me, and there

are many adversaries.

1 Corinthians 16:9, ESV

P aul the apostle is the embodiment of a glory carrier. We read about Paul's amazing journeys throughout the book of Acts. The one that most strikes me is Paul's journey to Ephesus in Acts 19–20. I believe we can take what happened through Paul in Ephesus and treat it as a prototype for what God is going to do through glory carriers in the end times.

I can imagine Paul as he was almost at the end of his three year stay at Ephesus summarizing what he felt in his letter to the Corinthians by saying, "A great and effectual door had opened to me" (1 Corinthians 16:9). What was this great and effectual door?

Paul's first trip to Ephesus was brief with little to no resistance. During his first trip, the people of the city welcomed him and wanted to hear more of the Gospel. Surprisingly this did not motivate Paul to stay seeing as he left soon after he arrived.

Ironically, when Paul wrote about an open door, he wasn't speaking about the favor of man on his first visit. The open door Paul spoke of came by way of many adversaries and was in reference to the power of God being released the second time he visited. (1 Corinthians 16:9)

This door I am speaking of was foreshadowed in Jacob's ladder and hinted at when Jesus spoke to Nathaniel about angels ascending and descending upon the Son of Man. Notice, Jesus said angels would ascend and descend upon a man and not a place. We know Jesus was speaking about himself but He also serves as an example of what we can walk in today. Jesus showed us that men and women are called to be bridges between heaven and earth. Paul experienced this bridge in his spirit while in Ephesus. (Genesis 28:10-17; John 1:51)

Paul, in fact, had so much heavenly power flowing through him that he prayed God would strengthen him to withstand the powerful manifestation of Christ in his heart. "That He would grant you, according to the riches of His glory, to be strengthened with power through His Spirit in the inner man, so that Christ may dwell in your hearts through faith" (Ephesians 3:16–17). This heavenly river of Christ was so strong in Paul that it soaked his clothing with an anointing that healed the sick and delivered demons. (Acts 19)

Paul was the door by which Heaven invaded earth. Let's look at some of the things that happened in Ephesus during Paul's three-year stay. (Acts 19:10–20:1)

1. All who dwelt in Asia heard the word of the Lord

2. Unusual miracles were wrought by the hands of Paul

3. Clothes from Paul's body were distributed throughout the city and brought healing and deliverance to whomever they touched

4. The fear of the Lord fell on the city

5. The name of the Lord Jesus was magnified

6. Many believed and confessed their deeds

7. There was a transfer of wealth from the wicked to the righteous

8. Many who practiced magic arts burned their books, which were valued at 50,000 silver pieces

9. The Word of the Lord grew mightily and prevailed

There was a massive shift for Kingdom advancement when this door opened up in Paul's spirit. Let's look a little closer at what happened with Paul in Ephesus as most of what we see was first birthed in the Spirit.

Chapter Three

PAUL'S VICTORIES IN THE SPIRIT

If according to man I fought wild beasts in Ephesus, what is

the profit to me?

1 Corinthians 15:32, BLB

Just as Jesus wrestled with the Devil in the wilderness and came out doing signs and wonders, Paul also wrestled with demons in Ephesus and came out victorious. The wrestling Paul overcame in Ephesus was a wrestling against his identity. Paul was able to stand firm in who he was even when the demonic tried to convince him otherwise. After the Devil was unable to convince Paul he was someone other than a Son of Glory the entire region shifted. When we learn who we are, we then are able to operate out of the power within us.

As Paul pondered the beasts he wrestled with in Ephesus, he wrote, "we wrestle not against flesh and blood, but against principalities, against powers, against the rulers of the darkness of this world, against spiritual wickedness in high places" (Ephesians 6:12). Paul pointed to a reality beyond the natural.

Paul provides his readers a description of what is necessary to fight this battle, and he calls it the Armor of God. Paul speaks about this armor as different aspects of our inheritance in Christ. Armor, by definition, is something that protects. When we think about how we approach spiritual warfare, we might think more often about how we are to attack the enemy. In reality, the truest way to find victory in the midst of spiritual battles is to understand that your defense is the foundational element of understanding who you are in Christ. If Paul and Jesus didn't understand who they were, they wouldn't have been able to stand against the enemies assault on their identities. The Enemy's attacks on your identity is always an attempt to derail the authority you have as a new creation in Christ.

Once we are planted in our identities, we can "be strong in the Lord and in the power of His might" (Ephesians 6:10, KJV). In giving us the armor of God, Paul gave us a set of parameters that will allow the heart to carry a sustained flow of God's presence. When we understand and meditate on the armor, it sets us up to be glory carriers.

The first piece of armor to put on is Truth. This is central to our ability to stand against the schemes of the enemy. The enemy is the accuser of the brethren and father of all lies. The Bible tells us in John 14:6 that Jesus himself is truth. In order for us to be grounded in truth, we need to be grounded in Christ.

When we are grounded in Him, we then are able to tell the difference between a truth and a lie. Even more important than knowing the truth is allowing the truth to know you. Paul writes to Timothy that, "...the Lord knows those who are his" (2 Timothy 2:19, BSB). The word "knows" in this passage is *gino* in the Greek. Its equivalent in Hebrew is *yada*. The word *yada* is used when Adam knew Eve in the Garden. These words express an intimate knowing. When we allow Christ to know us, the intimacy we experience builds eternal truth within us.

One of the best ways we can allow God to know us is by receiving His love. Once we surrender to His love and open ourselves up to His truth, we will be fortified in our identities. When we are filled with His truth, the enemy will have no place in us.

As you commune with Holy Spirit He will help "guide you into all the truth" (John 16:13, BSB). God's ability to lead us to truth is always more powerful than the enemy's attempt to deceive us. When we lean into our relationship with the Holy Spirit, we lean into the one who guides us to truth Himself. (John 14:30; 1 John 5:18)

The next piece of armor is the Breastplate of Righteousness. Beware: this is where the enemy tries to trip up the saints. Righteousness simply means, right standing with God. The enemy will try and make you believe that you need to obtain or earn your own righteousness; however, the Bible tells us that we already possess the righteousness of God in Christ Jesus.

This righteousness is perfect and there is nothing we can do to improve it. Our new man has already been created in, "true Righteousness and Holiness" (Ephesians 4:24).

When the enemy tells you that you are not worthy or good enough to stand in God's presence, you can stand in truth and declare, "He made Him who knew no sin to be sin on our behalf, so that we might become the righteousness of God in Him" (2 Corinthians 5:21). As we declare the truth of God's Word, the enemy must back off and accept his defeat.

The next defensive piece is the Shield of Faith. The enemy may try to plant doubt in our minds as to God's existence. Many fiery darts that are launched against us are thoughts that try to exalt themselves above the knowledge of God. Faith is rightly pictured as a shield because when you choose faith over a lie, it blocks doubt and unbelief. The Bible tells us that Jesus is the "... author and perfecter of faith" (Hebrews 12:2). Walking with faith is synonymous with walking with Jesus. He is our perfect example, who only did what He saw the Father do. Jesus walked in such a strong relational connection of faith with the Father that it protected Him from the darts of the wicked one. (2 Corinthians 10:2; John 5:19)

The next defensive piece is the Helmet of Salvation. This is the knowledge of what Christ accomplished for you on the cross. If the enemy can distort this information, he can disrupt your whole life. This knowledge consists of how we partake in Christ's death, burial, and resurrection. It is rightly a helmet, protecting the head and mind because the mind is one of the main areas the enemy tries to attack.

The word salvation means to be saved, delivered, and preserved. There is something that happened at salvation where, "If anyone is in Christ he is a new creation, the old has passed away. Behold, the new has come!" (2 Corinthians 5:17, ESV). In Christ we are new creations who were saved from stony, hardened, sin-sickened hearts and given soft, holy, loving hearts. When the enemy tries to bring up the past, we can remind him that "It is no longer I who live, but Christ lives in me" (Galatians 2:20).

Paul encouraged us to remain standing after the Devil attempts to plant a lie. Just as Jesus and Paul stood on truth, we also are called to follow suit. Our job is to rest in the knowledge of our inheritance in Him. Paul walked in this understanding, which disarmed the enemies attempt to wrestle lies into his life.

Once we realize that most of what we do in warfare is rest in truth, striving in battle ceases. When warfare is done at the table, feasting on God's nature, celebration and triumph is our portion. Christ's victory allows us to relax and overflow with an anointing that crushes the enemy. He put all principalities and powers on public display, revealing to all that they are now disarmed in the light of His legal victory on the cross. Christ's authority demands submission from the enemy. Paul carried this weight of co-identity with Christ and rendered the demonic realm helpless under the authority of His glory-filled son-ship.

Truth, righteousness, faith, and salvation are all aspects of our inheritance in Christ. Paul tells us to meditate on these attributes to fortify our identities in Christ. As we learn who we are, it protects our identities and sustains the flow of glory in our lives. In the next section we will look at a few offensive strategies Paul implemented in Ephesus.

Part Two:
ADVANCING THE KINGDOM

Chapter Four:

DISMANTLING THE DEMONIC

The kingdom of the world has become the kingdom of our Lord and of his Christ, and he shall reign forever and ever.

Revelation 11:15, ESV

A good team is made up of both a good defense and a great offense. Spiritual warfare is about understanding our identities and also learning how to flow with the Father. Jesus only did what He saw the Father do. The Father is our offensive coordinator, and He won't stop "until his enemies be made a footstool for his feet" (Hebrews 10:13). As we allow the glory to flow through our lives, we advance God's kingdom and overcome spiritual forces of darkness.

The open door for Paul was a release of Heavenly authority that dismantled demonic powers in the region of Ephesus. I believe the door Paul experienced was a partial fulfillment of Revelation 3:8–9: "Behold, I have put before you an open door which no one can shut...I will cause those of the synagogue of Satan, who say that they are Jews and are not, but lie—I will make them come and bow down at your feet, and make them know that I have loved you."

The door in Paul's spirit caused an overturning of the kingdom of darkness and allowed a harvest for the kingdom of Light. Many in Ephesus gave up their devotion to Satan so that they could serve God. "And many of those who practiced magic brought their books together and began burning them in the sight of everyone; and they counted up the price of them and found it fifty thousand pieces of silver" (Acts 19:19–20).

The level of authority we walk in is connected to our relationship with Jesus. As we commune and fellowship with the Holy Spirit, God's authoritative glory and fragrance fills the atmospheres around us.

A great example that provides contrast is that of the event when a group of Jewish exorcists wanted to replicate Paul's deliverance ministry and ran into a bit of a problem. These exorcists tried to cast a demon out of a man in the name of Jesus, and this is what the demon said: "I recognize Jesus, and I know about Paul, but who are you?" (Acts 19:15). These exorcists, who were called the sons of Sceva, had no recognition in the spiritual realm because they had no relationship with Jesus. It doesn't matter what our lip service and antics are when it comes to carrying the authoritative weight of Heaven. Paul could stand against the enemy because he was connected with Christ relationally.

Paul's spiritual identification held up because his "citizenship is in heaven" (Philippians 3:20). As a citizen, Paul carried the benefits, protection, and backing of another realm superior to the natural. The glory that flowed through Paul placed authoritative weight on the words he spoke and the atmosphere he walked in.

Sometimes, no words even need to be spoken for a demon to flee; they leave simply because the glory of God. There are other times when we must call for deliverance with our voices, activating God's power. When a demon is spiritually discerned by the Lord through you, it gives you the right and authority to speak to it and command it to leave.

Once the enemy realized he couldn't lie to Paul, he planted lies in the people around him. This was the second phase of the enemy's attempt to hinder Paul's identity. If he can't influence your mind, heart, or emotions directly he will influence others who are more open and vulnerable to identity theft. He will then use these individuals to speak negatively about you.

As much as God prophesies life over us through His people, the enemy attempts to prophesy death. If you value the opinion of man above the opinion of God, you will open a door for the enemy's influence. Paul didn't allow the opinion of others to move him; his identity was so grounded that when people came against his life, he didn't sway.

This led to the third phase of the enemy's attack, an all-out physical assault on Paul's life. The Devil possessed mobs in Ephesus in an attempt to physically kill Paul. Even though there was massive revival in Ephesus for three years, the enemy made a last-minute effort to remove Paul from the city.

This is the thorn Paul refers to in 2 Corinthians 12:7–12. A thorn in the flesh was referred to in the old testament as a group of people that were detrimental to one's own safety. Paul had this happening as people came against him everywhere he went. Paul was sensitive to the spirit realm and understood this to be a demonic attack. Paul describes the thorn as a "messenger of Satan." (Numbers 33:55)

The people who were influenced by the enemy were so intoxicated with demonic confusion that they didn't know why they were rioting. "So then, some were shouting one thing and some another, for the assembly was in confusion and the majority did not know for what reason they had come together" (Acts 19:32). In 2 Corinthians 12:10, Paul explained this thorn as mistreatments, persecutions, and difficulties he'd suffered for Christ. Jesus tells us that, "The kingdom of Heaven suffers violence, and the violent take it by force" (Matthew 11:12). This statement was spoken in the context of John the Baptist being beheaded. The word of God never promises that we are safe from persecution in this age.

Paul realized he couldn't have authority over persecution or pray it away.

When he did ask for it to go away the Lord responded with, "My grace is sufficient for you, my power is perfected in weakness" (2 Corinthians 12:9, BSB). God allows us to thrive even when the enemy thinks he is the one winning. After Paul realized he couldn't get away from persecution, he embraced this weakness and pressed into the high calling of God.

Paul used this thorn as a buffer, "to keep me from exalting myself" (2 Corinthians 12:7). This, in turn, opened up even more revelation and encounters with the Lord for Paul.

The question we should ask ourselves is this: If God was moving on a massive scale in Ephesus, how did the enemy still have access to maneuver some people in the city?

Chapter Five:
TRANSFER OF WEALTH

Men, you know that from this business we have our wealth. And you see and hear that not only in Ephesus but in almost all of Asia this Paul has persuaded and turned away a great many people, saying that gods made with hands are not gods. And there is danger not only that this trade of ours may come into disrepute but also that the temple of the great goddess Artemis may be counted as nothing.
Acts 19:23–27, ESV

During Paul's stay at Ephesus, many people were making their living on temple prostitution and idol worship. As the Devil sought those whom he might devour in the city of Ephesus, he found the ones in charge of idol worship and prostitution to be easy prey. (1 Peter 5:8)

The book of Ephesians tells us not to give the Devil a foothold. This phrase is used to indicate what happens in the spirit when a door is opened. As the Devil places his metaphorical foot in someone, he is then able to bring movement to their life. The Devil found a foothold in these leaders and took "them captive to his will" (2 Timothy 2:26, BSB).

These leaders became vulnerable to the enemy because they agreed with fear after losing many customers to Paul's preaching. Instead of buying idols and paying for prostitutes, people spent their money giving to the church. This was a case of wicked spending transferred to righteous giving.

How would this look like today if sex slavery, prostitution, and drugs all became things people no longer wanted or spent money on? The millions and billions going into these places would be transferred, working to Kingdom advancement.

As part of the city was experiencing supernatural revival and submitting to the power of God, there was a part of the population who sided with fear, which led to the spreading of the gospel message geographically. When the church is persecuted, the Lord is still able to use it to advance His kingdom.

Paul wrote while in prison that, "the word of God is not imprisoned" (2 Timothy 2:9). God's word is so powerful nothing in all of the universe can box it in. Let's look at how the word impacted Ephesus and the various ways it affects creation.

Chapter Six:
THE WORD OF GOD

The grass withers, the flower fades, But the word of our God stands forever.

Isaiah 40:8

The active preaching of the word in Ephesus caused most of the principalities in the region to lose power. As people's hearts turned to Christ, people learned about their true identities and let go of darkness.

When Paul preached the word, he disrupted demonic forces in the spirit. The word of God is extremely powerful, specifically in the message of Jesus Christ and His crucifixion. This message of salvation will open the unbeliever into the new reality of life in God.

The one thing the enemy uses massive resources on is blocking the Gospel of Jesus Christ. "The god of this world has blinded the minds of the unbelieving so that they might not see the light of the gospel of the glory of Christ, who is the image of God." (2 Corinthians 4:4). The mind has a demonic blinding on it until it's penetrated by the light of the glorious Gospel.

The enemy does not want the world to know the Gospel. He does all he can to hinder the message of Jesus Christ and Him crucified because this message is what frees people from sin and darkness. When the Gospel is preached, the light turns on, and when the light turns on, people are able to respond to the presentation of a relationship with Christ.

Paul based his life work on being "determined to know nothing among you except Jesus Christ, and Him crucified" (1 Corinthians 2:2). Paul was committed to the message of Christ. This was another reason the enemy wanted to end his life. Paul said, "For I am not ashamed of the Gospel, for it is the power of God for salvation to everyone who believes, to the Jew first and also to the Greek" (Romans 1:16). Paul calls the Gospel the power of God to save. This power is what penetrates the demonic blinding of the enemy and releases people into the freedom of sonship.

Throughout Paul's letters there is a consistent theme regarding the importance of the Gospel. "How then will they call on Him in whom they have not believed? How will they believe in Him whom they have not heard? And how will they hear without a preacher? How will they preach unless they are sent?" (Romans 10:14).

He asked the Ephesian Church to pray for him, "That utterance may be given to me in the opening of my mouth, to make known with boldness the mystery of the gospel" (Ephesians 6:19). Paul wanted to be able to speak the word in boldness and without compromise.

He understood that this was his mission and submitted that he needed help in fulfilling it.

Once we hear the story of Christ and how it connects to each of us, we can then respond to a relationship with Jesus. He has welcomed us into union with Himself that frees us from sin and saves us for eternity. This is the message Paul gave to the world around him; he desired that others might see the image of the invisible God.

The word of God is also mentioned as an offensive weapon in Ephesians six. One of the primary ways of advancing God's kingdom is through His Word. The Bible calls the Word a two-edged sword that is effective against the demonic spirits outside and the thought patterns inside: "For the word of God is living and active and sharper than any two-edged sword, and piercing as far as the division of soul and spirit, of both joints and marrow, and able to judge the thoughts and intentions of the heart" (Hebrews 4:12). When we allow the word of God to fully possess us, it opens us up to seeing our pure identities. The word allows us to discern the inner workings of our DNA and manifest the fullness of our personalities and gifting's in Christ.

In the beginning, God spoke and it was. As God speaks through us, atmospheres change for kingdom advancement. By one word, people will be healed; by one song, massive deliverance will take place. As we speak the words spoken to us from the Father, all of Hell will not be able to stand against Heaven's power. Stadiums will be filled with worshipers making declarations laced with heaven's glory, releasing supernatural power to flow into regions.

The Word is not only powerful when we declare it, but it's also, as the book of Hebrews tells us, the very fabric that holds the universe together, "upholding all things by the word of His power" (Hebrews 1:3). The word of God is the most stable force in all of the created order.

Paul spoke to the Ephesian elders and gave them his last address before heading to Jerusalem. Paul wanted to give his best advice, knowing he wouldn't see these leaders again, so he started by saying, "I commend you to God and to the word of His grace, which is able to build you up and to give you the inheritance among all those who are sanctified" (Acts 20:32). Paul drew the elders' attention to the word of God. Paul knew that this very word would give these elders an inheritance that would carry into the age to come.

Isaiah tells us the Word of God will stand forever. This means that what God has said will endure through the fire at the end of the age. God made a promise to Abraham, "for all the land which you see, I will give it to you and to your descendants forever" (Genesis 13:15; Isaiah 40:3). God made another promise concerning Israel, "But Judah will be inhabited forever And Jerusalem for all generations" (Joel 3:20). When we trust in God's Word, we trust in a substance that is everlasting. God has woven His eternal Word into mankind and into the earth He has given them.

John said, "In the beginning was the Word, and the Word was with God, and the Word was God" (John 1:1). The Bible tells us that God Himself is the Word. This word became flesh in Jesus and is now in bodily form seated at the right hand of the Father. We see an example of the word living on after death in Jesus. Jesus is our example of what a resurrected man in a resurrected body looks like. When Christ resurrected, He didn't vanish into thin air and become some ethereal being that we can't relate too. Jesus, in His resurrected body, was still able to eat and be touched by His disciples.

Jesus is our example of the Word of God enduring into the age to come. Jesus has gone before us to make a way for mankind to step into a new age of life. Jesus is now seated at the right hand of the Father, waiting for the appointed time to return to earth and reign from Jerusalem. The resurrected Christ will come to earth to reign and finalize the restoration of all things.

Chapter Seven:
THE GOSPEL OF PEACE

The God of peace will soon crush Satan under your feet.

Romans 16:20

Another item Paul mentions in Ephesians six are the shoes of the Gospel of Peace. Peace is a powerful weapon that crushes Satan and advances God's kingdom. Peace is not only a concept but also a presence. A lot of scripture connects peace with God Himself.

When Jesus spoke peace into a storm, His internal reality became external through the declaration. Creation itself responded to the Creator. When Jesus said "my peace I give to you," the same peace in Jesus that calmed the raging storm is the same peace inside of us right now. (John 14:27)

Ultimately what the Bible tells us is that the disruption and chaos we have brought to this earth through our rebellion against God will be replaced by restoration and peace. By this peace, order will be re-established and mankind will once again walk with God in the cool of the day. This peace was a part of Jesus's perfect spirit. He was the first one to ever be of perfect order after the fall. Jesus began a new race of people who carry in them the order of Heaven.

As we preach the Gospel of peace to all creation, God's glory invades the earth. When people come into agreement with the word they are set free along with the atmosphere around them. When we learn who we are through the gospel we answer the call of Christ to join in on the restoration of all things. Mankind will ultimately decide the atmospheres that saturate our cities by what we come into agreement with. When we agree to the value of our identities, darkness is destroyed and glory is released.

We have authority through Christ to take back what was originally given to us and partner with God in the restoration of all things. Psalm 115:19 tells us that "The highest heavens belong to the LORD, but the earth he has given to mankind." It is our job to properly steward what God has given us in the earth by creating heavenly atmospheres.

As we implement Christ's peace in the earth, Satanic plans of fear are crushed. The kingdom itself is "righteousness, peace, and joy in the Holy Spirit" (Romans 14:17). When we release the peace and glory of God, it allows others to be set free from fear. As people come into agreement with God's Word and release peace, atmospheres will shift for kingdom advancement.

Chapter Eight:
RESTORATION AND RECONCILIATION

For he himself is our peace, who has made the two groups one and has destroyed the barrier, the dividing wall of hostility.

Ephesians 2:14

eace will play a part in the reconciliation of relationships. As we experience the peace of God in our hearts, we can then connect with that same peace in others. It's one thing to have the glory flow through one person, but it's another when the glory flows through two or more who are united in Christ. In Ephesians 2:14, Paul spoke about the mystery now revealed that the Jew and Gentile are both welcomed into the family of God.

Whether Jew or Gentile, slave or free, we are all one in Christ. When Paul was in Ephesus, he wrote to the Corinthian church that, "God reconciled us to Himself through Christ and gave us the ministry of reconciliation" (2 Corinthians 5:18). Just as God reconciled us to Himself, we are called to minister this reconciliation to the earth.

Having God as our peace through the finished work of the cross allows us to be one with the body. This connection with the church causes an acceleration of God's presence that will shift atmospheres for kingdom advancement. When we are rightly connected to one another, the manifestation of the nature of God in the earth intensifies. When the church decides to stop fighting with each other and begins connecting as a family, God's glory will manifest.

The prophet Amos foretold of a time when the tabernacle of David would be rebuilt. The tabernacle of David was a place where all people were able to come together and worship God. The apostle James stood before the Jerusalem council and quoted Amos 9:11 to answer a dispute on whether the Gentiles should be allowed into the church. "After these things I will return, And I will rebuild the tabernacle of David which has fallen, And I will rebuild its ruins, And I will restore it, So that the rest of mankind may seek the Lord" (Acts 15:16–18).

As we reconcile with one another in the presence of the Lord and do life together, the fullness of God's character will be on display. We will see the joining of races, genders, denominations, and generations. The walls that block intimacy will be broken down, and we will be united as one family. The restoration of all things will carry with it the restoration of God's family

Part of what happened in Ephesus during the open door was people turning from their evil deeds. This plays a major role in reconciliation. A father coming to his son to acknowledge the wrong that he has done to him. A daughter owning up to the bad things she has done in her relationships. In essence, when the Holy Spirit moves on this scale, our hearts become sensitive to what grieves the Holy Spirit.

Paul had insight into the things that grieve Him. Each item listed in Ephesians 4:30–32 has to do with the way we treat ourselves and others. Paul lists bitterness, wrath, anger, clamor, slander, and malice as things we need to put off. As an alternative, Paul's tells us to "Be kind to one another, tenderhearted, forgiving each other, just as God in Christ also has forgiven you." This is key to reconciliation. We can see from this list that the Holy Spirit is very sensitive about the way we treat one another.

When we treat others poorly, we quench the flow of the Holy Spirit and glory from our lives. Creation will respond to either the kindness or bitterness of our hearts. When we respond with kindness, we play a part in restoring everything around us. Our kind acts and works are actually things that will be sustained into the age to come. The quality of relationship we have with one another will determine the quality of God's presence that manifests in our corporate gatherings.

Paul speaks strongly about the way we connect with one another when he talks about the revelation he received from Christ personally about the last supper. He called the church of Corinth out by saying, "I do not praise you, because you come together not for the better but for the worse" (1 Corinthians 11:17, BLB). Paul had reports of the church having divisions and fractions as they came together to take communion.

In contrast, he told them the position of Christ. "For I received from the Lord that which I also delivered to you, that the Lord Jesus in the night in which He was betrayed took bread; and when He had given thanks, He broke it and said, "This is My body, which is for you; do this in remembrance of Me" (1 Corinthians 11:23). Paul gave the example of Christ who gave of Himself even in the midst of betrayal. He encouraged them to come together and be grateful rather than selfish and entitled.

The people were not taking time to sit back and reflect on the finished work, and they took advantage of the food and filled their selfish bodies, unaware of the people around them. Paul was pointing them to a reality of being tender toward one another and recognizing each other as being a part of one another.

When Christ died, He created a way for us to have a connection with each other, a connection that has not been fully seen in all of history. Jesus actually said that an indicator of discipleship would be the church's love for one another, "I have loved you, so you must love one another, By this all men will know that you are My disciples, if you love one another" (John 13:35, BSB).

If we are to form a fully functioning church, we must honor, respect, and love one another. Each person has a different role in the manifestation of the fullness of God's nature in the earth. When we learn about the nature of our unique identities and understand how to flow with one another, we can then implement the action plan God wants to accomplish in the earth, manifesting His glory and shifting the very atmosphere of the earth and the heavens. "His purpose was that now, through the church, the manifold wisdom of God should be made known to the rulers and authorities in the heavenly realms" (Ephesians 3:10 BSB). The manifold wisdom is that the Jew and Gentile can become one in Christ. In other words, mankind now has a bridge, made possible through Christ, to become one family.

The enemy mocks God for thinking He will have a people who are truly united in love. The enemy has become overconfident about his schemes that bring division to homes, churches, and relationships. As the Church becomes one, the powers and authorities in the heavenlies will be astounded.

This will be a reality for the end-time church: we will walk in the fulfillment of Christ's prayer, "That they may all be one; even as You, Father, are in Me and I in You, that they also may be in Us, so that the world may believe that You sent Me" (John 17:21, BSB). When the church agrees with Christ's heart cry, we will walk in a unity that reveals the nature of God to the world around us. We will be so united in Christ that the rage of Satan and all his schemes will not be able to divide one brother from another. This will completely baffle the world and the demonic forces behind the world system.

Chapter Nine

HEALING THE LAND THROUGH RECONCILIATION

Behold, I am going to send you Elijah the prophet before the

coming of the great and terrible day of the LORD. "He will restore the

hearts of the fathers to their children and the hearts of the children to

their fathers, so that I will not come and smite the land with a curse.

Malachi 4:5–6

As we turn our hearts to one another in kindness, our families and land will be restored. Notice in Malachi's prophecy how the restoration of families is directly tied to the health of the land. As this reconciliation happens between husband and wife, black and white, father and son, the result will manifest in the restoration of the air we breathe and ground we stand on.

Part of the reason Eden was a paradise was because Adam and Eve had a paradise inside of them and between them. Before the fall, there was absolutely no shame in their relationship. They were the original glory carriers that walked in the paradise of the Garden. As soon as this inner paradise was disrupted, they had to be removed from the garden because they were no longer compatible and needed salvation.

Notice also how God's commandment, "Honor your father and your mother," was tied to land, "that you may live long in the land the LORD your God is giving you" (Exodus 20:12). This promise indicates that in order to live in "the land the LORD your God is giving you," honor is required.

In Adam and Eve's case, the lack of honor and trust with the Father resulted in their removal from the land. Broken relationship equals broken land; restored, healthy relationships equal restored healthy atmospheres. In order for our land to be restored, we need massive reconciliation of families and marriages that look like Jesus.

Godly marriage relationships are going to play a major role in the restoration of all things. Paul had a powerful revelation about marriage that he shared with the Ephesian church. He likened the relationship of a husband and wife to our personal relationship with Christ. Paul tells husbands to model loving their wives after the way Christ loves the church. A husband-and-wife relationship is the closest possible union you can have with anyone in this life. This is what Jesus has with us. In essence, a married couple should be a mirrored manifestation of the way God loves us.

God is going to raise up marriages that carry Eden levels of glory where there is no sin and a shared relational connection with the presence of God. Adam and Eve didn't have the authority to change the garden, but we do. These glory marriages are going to restore the very land they come in contact with as they honor, trust, and love one another. There will be an exponential release of glory in marriages that will shatter the fibers of evil in the land. Marriages between a husband and wife will be highlighted at the end of the age along with the church's identity as a bride.

When a bride calls out for her husband, she cries out from a place of passionate desire and love for her beloved. The core of her cry comes from a place of simply wanting to be with him. Revelation 22:17 tells us that at the end of the age, "The Spirit and the bride say, 'Come!'" This tells us that we are not going to call out to God as an army for its general, or as a slave for his master, or even as a son for his father. We will still hold to all of these identities, but scripture tells us that at the end of the age we will call out to Him as a bride. One of the reasons Christ is going to return is out of response to a bride who is filled with fiery love for Him.

The Song of Solomon describes the love between a husband and wife as a fire that cannot be quenched. "Set me as a seal upon thy heart, As a seal upon thine arm: For love is strong as death; Jealousy is cruel as Sheol; The flashes thereof are flashes of fire, A very flame of Jehovah. Many waters cannot quench love, Neither can floods drown it: If a man would give all the substance of his house for love, He would utterly be contemned" (Song of Solomon 8:6-7, ASV). This is the kind of love we get to experience with God.

The love of God is, by far, the most powerful force in all the universe. As we approach the end of the age, this fiery love will increase as God's heart burns for His bride. This fire will be so powerful that it will consume everything that is not love at the end of the age.

This fire will not only flow from us as His love encounters us but it will also come upon us. The fire from God will pour out all over the earth, and the fire from us will simultaneously do the same. God is very serious about relationship and that will manifest in fiery passion at the end of the age.

Chapter Ten

IN THE WORLD BUT NOT OF IT

If you were of the world, the world would love you as its own; but

because you are not of the world, but I chose you out of the world,

therefore the world hates you.

John 15:19

Throughout history, the problem with mankind has been our incompatibility with God. After the fall, we disqualified ourselves from compatibility with the garden and His glory. Christ came to bridge the gap and make a way for us to enter into the holy place. Now, we can boldly come before God, who the Bible calls an "all-consuming fire" (Hebrews 12:29, ISV). How do we remain compatible with a fire that consumes everything that is not of Him? (Hebrews 4:16)

As we experienced the new birth, we are no longer of the world but of Christ. "May I never boast except in the cross of our Lord Jesus Christ, through which the world has been crucified to me, and I to the world" (Galatians 6:14). When we died with Christ, we died to the world, which the Bible defines as, "the lust of the flesh, the lust of the eyes, and the pride of life" (1 John 2:16).

Every unhealthy attachment with this world system will be burned away and consumed. Everything we build based on the lust of the flesh, lust of the eyes, and the pride of life will not stand the test of the fiery love of God.

John contrasts the love of God with the world by saying, "Do not love the world or the things in the world. If anyone loves the world, the love of the Father is not in him" (1 John 2:15). In Jesus' prayer to the Father, He stated, "They are not of the world, even as I am not of it" (John 17:16).

The Book of Revelation personifies the world system as a harlot that rules over the kings of the earth. This harlot is made up of the forces and powers behind the lust of the flesh, lust of the eyes, and the pride of life. The Book of Revelation tells us that this harlot will be judged with fire: "For this reason in one day...she will be burned up with fire; for the Lord God who judges her is strong. And the kings of the earth, who committed acts of immorality and lived sensuously with her, will weep and lament over her when they see the smoke of her burning" (Revelation 18:8–9).

Many people who invest their hearts and emotions into the world system will suffer loss. "If any man's work is burned up, he will suffer loss; but he himself will be saved, yet so as through fire" (1 Corinthians 3:15). When people build according to the world system, they are simply building with chaff that will be consumed at the end of the age.

The closer we get to the end of the age, the more acclimated to His fire we must become. When our internal reality is tethered to the Father's heart, the fire of His love is enjoyable, not scary or torturous. When we begin to love the things He loves, the fire becomes a part of who we are rather than an enemy of our desires. As His fire increases, selfishness is burned away and pure love emerges from the ashes. As the fire of God comes to those who believe, it will remove the dross and bring forth the purity within us. Our hearts will be rewarded as the fire sifts through everything that is not love.

This is what happened in Ephesus; a spiritual fire of revival burned through the hearts of the Ephesians to the point where they were "confessing and telling their deeds" (Acts 19:18). When the fire touches people's lives, it accelerates the process of change that is necessary in acclimation to His nature. People can choose to either acknowledge and repent of their sin or go deeper into it.

The flame will bring out the motives of man's heart and judge wickedness; simultaneously, God will reward the treasures of love that we've accumulated throughout this life. "Therefore do not go on passing judgment before the time, but wait until the Lord comes who will both bring to light the things hidden in the darkness and disclose the motives of men's hearts; and then each man's praise will come to him from God" (1 Corinthians 1:5).

We can experience right now the same fire that we will experience at the end of the age. He's the same God, yesterday, today, and forever; an "all-consuming fire" (Hebrews 12:29). A big step in becoming acclimated to His flame is to get baptized with the Holy Spirit and fire. "I baptize you with water for repentance. But after me comes one who is more powerful than I, whose sandals I am not worthy to carry. He will baptize you with the Holy Spirit and fire" (Matthew 3:11).

One of the first things Paul did when he came to Ephesus was make sure the disciples were filled with the Holy Spirit. In order to enter into any level of spiritual warfare, Paul knew that to be "filled with the Spirit" was essential. "Paul had laid his hands upon them, the Holy Spirit came on them, and they began speaking with tongues and prophesying. There were in all about twelve men" (Acts 19:6-7).

Paul trained twelve disciples in the truth of their identities, who helped him shake the city of Ephesus. He needed a united group of believers to help with the exponential release of God's glory. These twelve with Paul were able to release the glory of God in the region, which resulted in a shift of the entire city.

Being filled with the Holy Spirit and His fire is essential to becoming acclimated to His nature (Ephesians 5:18; Acts 19:6–7). His fire is a friend to believers and an enemy to the world system. Allow His fire to fill you and flow through you!

Part Three:
THE END of the AGE

Chapter Eleven:
THE FIRE OF HEAVEN

For when they maintain this, it escapes their notice that by the word of
God the heavens existed long ago and the earth was formed out of water
and by water, through which the world at that time was destroyed,
being flooded with water. But by His word the present heavens and
earth are being reserved for fire, kept for the day of judgment and
destruction of ungodly men.

2 Peter 3:5–7

It's important to note how the Bible makes a distinction between the earth before the flood and the earth after. Peter states that the world before the flood was destroyed, "at that time" by water. The word "destroyed" in this passage doesn't mean a complete removal of the entirety of earth's matter but rather the removal of the unrighteous people on the planet.

Similarly the fire at the end of the age will bring a cleansing and will consume everything that is not aligned with righteousness in the earth and also in the heavens. This fire, unlike the flood, will not only bring cleansing to the people but also to anything in the earth or the heavens that are stained by agents of wickedness and their influence. The fire of God's passionate heart will restore mankind and the created order back to Himself. In the meantime God is waiting for His family to grow and mature in manifesting the fullness of what the Bible promises.

This flame will not fully destroy the earth, as the Bible promises, "Generations come and generations go, but the earth remains forever" (Ecclesiastes 1:4). This all-consuming fire will birth the earth into a new phase of purity with a cleansed heavens. The natural and spiritual realm will be completely undefiled by wickedness. This cleansing will create a beautiful atmosphere whereby Christ can rule and usher in the finalization of the restoration of all things at the end of the age.

In order to understand this fire we need to first understand how the spirit realm affects the natural. Jude describes his experience as, "hating even the garment polluted by the flesh." (Jude 1:23). Jude indicates that sin can seep into the natural realm. Paul showed us that glory can become tangible in the clothes we wear. People distributed Paul's clothes from his body and sent them throughout Ephesus because they brought healing and deliverance to whomever they touched. The glory was so strong in Peter's life that people could be healed just by being in close proximity to him. The woman with the issue of blood was healed by simply touching the hem of Jesus' garment. These are all examples of the spirit realm becoming tangible. (Malachi 4; Acts 5:5; Acts 19)

The Bible gives us evidence of what this fire looks like. "'For behold, the day is coming, burning like a furnace; and all the arrogant and every evildoer will be chaff; and the day that is coming will set them ablaze,' says the LORD of hosts, 'so that it will leave them neither root nor branch" (Malachi 4:1). The word "them" in this verse is important because it implies ownership of the land with a specific people group. In this case, it is connected to the wicked of the land. As some parts of the earth get cleansed and consumed because of wickedness, other parts will be cleansed with fire yet not consumed because of holiness.

An example of parts of the earth that are on fire yet not consumed is that of the burning bush. Moses saw a bush that was on fire yet not consumed. The reason the bush was not consumed was because of the holiness that saturated the land. God told Moses to take off his shoes for the land itself was holy. How was the land itself holy? The land was holy because of the One who dwelt in it. There was no conflict between the land and this heavenly fire.

In the book of Daniel, Shadrach, Meshach, and Abednego, were thrown into a furnace as punishment and were not harmed. "But I see four men unbound, walking in the midst of the fire, and they are not hurt; and the appearance of the fourth is like a son of the gods" (Daniel 3:25, ESV). The three men were accompanied by a fourth man who kept them from being destroyed in the fire. The bush was not consumed because of the One who dwelt in the land, just as the men were not consumed because of the One who dwelt in the fire.

When we align our lives according to Christ, we align with the flame Himself.

The writer of Hebrews references this fire as a description of what will happen at the end of the age. "And His voice shook the earth then (referring to Mt. Sinai) but now He has promised, saying, 'YET ONCE MORE I WILL SHAKE NOT ONLY THE EARTH, BUT ALSO THE HEAVEN, This expression, "yet once more" denotes the removal of those things that can be shaken, as in <u>created things</u>, so that those things which cannot be shaken may remain. Therefore, since we receive a kingdom which cannot be shaken, let us show gratitude, by which we may offer to God an acceptable service with reverence and awe; for our God is a consuming fire" (Hebrews 12:26–29). The writer points us to the fact that God Himself is a consuming fire that will shake everything that is not kingdom.

The term "created things" in this passage speaks specifically about the works and creations of men and agents created by God. This consuming fire will consume every work of man and fallen angel that has partnered with the lust of the flesh, lust of the eyes, and the pride of life.

The fire will consume the systems that man has created on earth as well as the Devil's system, which were created in the heavens. The Book of Revelation depicts the world system as a "great city that rules over the kings of the earth" (Revelation 17: 18). This city is a demonic structure in the spirit that empowers the lust of the flesh, lust of the eyes, and the pride of life on earth. When people build according to this system, they are building with chaff.

Alternatively, the Bible talks about a city that cannot be shaken. Abraham saw this city, which had "foundations, whose architect and builder is God" (Hebrews 11:10). Abraham had a vision of the kingdom of God. When we build according to this system, we build according to a system that cannot be shaken. As we partner with God in relationship, we are building structures for eternity. More importantly, as you partner with God, He will mold and shape your heart into a beautiful, kind, and noble gem that will carry into the age to come.

This fire will cleanse and not consume areas where God's people saturate the land with holiness. Every time the fire is mentioned as that which destroys, it is attached to the wicked of the earth and their works. There will be a major conflict between the fire and anything that stands against God. Jesus told his disciples, "I have come to bring fire on the earth, and how I wish it were already kindled" (Luke 12:49). He didn't say this in a negative sense but with a heart to see the earth and heavens birthed into a new age of purity and love. God's fiery love will burn away all traces of things that hinder His heart.

Chapter Twelve:
WORKS THAT LAST

The earth and its works will be <u>burned</u> up.

2 Peter 3:10

In earlier manuscripts, they found that instead of the word "burned" they used "discovered." Essentially, what that tells us is that the fire will discover or reveal the works of the earth and men for what they are. This is the very nature of God, "Nothing in all creation is hidden from God's sight. Everything is uncovered and laid bare before the eyes of him to whom we must give account" (Hebrews 4:13).

In the same way that the fire will cleanse the motives of men's hearts, it will also cleanse the works we have built throughout history. "Their work will be shown for what it is, because the Day will bring it to light. It will be revealed with fire, and the fire will test the quality of each person's work. If what has been built survives, the builder will receive a reward" (1 Corinthians 3:13). There will be a reward for building lives and works that survive and remain. We are called to build ourselves, others, and systems that have eternal impact. What does it mean to build something that will last into the age to come?

When the Devil took Jesus to a high place, he took Him up to view the world and see the glory for each kingdom. "Again, the Devil took him to a very high mountain and showed him all the kingdoms of the world and their glory" (Matthew 4:8). This ultimately is what Jesus was promised from the Father. "I will make the nations your inheritance, the ends of the earth your possession" (Psalms 2:8). Jesus knew he shouldn't take the nations from the enemy out of convenience but instead wait to inherit them from the Father through relationship.

This is what He obtained through His death, burial, and resurrection. Now, all authority in heaven and earth has been given to him. The glory of the kingdoms of the earth now have the opportunity to re-align themselves with heaven and become conduits by which God's glory can invade earth.

We are not only called to be glory carriers individually but also corporately. The Lord has blueprints for organizations and ministries that will have their beginnings in this age and continue into the next. Eternal glory can be built in this life with the work we put our hearts to. A painting, a book, a system of teaching, all of these can be carried with us into the next age.

Any collaboration we have had with God to reach out to the lost, unloved, and broken of this world will be rewarded. The times where we had a choice to love our enemies and decided to partner with

God for the solution, these treasures will always be with us and will exude from our very beings. Many of us will be surprised by the way the Lord views and rewards our hearts at the end of the age. The age to come is not about sitting on a cloud with a harp. What we have stewarded with our gifts and hearts in this age will be the platform by which we continue into the next.

Part of a kingdom's glory is the level of excellence and creativity it displays. How much do you care about what God has given you? When you focus on the little things and spend time with creative excellence, you begin to step into the heart of the Creator. As we step into the heart of the Creator, glory begins to envelope our work. Solomon's kingdom had glory in it, the very attire of Solomon's servants took the Queen of Sheba's breath away.

As we pursue this excellence that brings glory to God, we must remember the most important form of excellence is love. If your outward display of excellence does not match your inward working of love, the excellence you are showing carries no weight in the spiritual realm. If you look like a prince on the outside but hate on the inside, the result will not be the same as someone who carries their heart well in love.

There will be organizations and ministries that carry love and display excellence and thus will reveal the glory of God to the nations. These structures can be so aligned with eternity that elements of their creative designs will live on into the next age. These works will be works that remain through the fire.

The day Christ returns will be a great day indeed for the sons of glory. This fire will cleanse the heavens and the earth, ushering in what the Bible calls the new heavens and the new earth. Christ will lead on earth as he fulfills the promise he made to David, that he "will have a descendant sitting on the throne of Israel forever" (Jeremiah 33:17). For the first time ever, we will have a true earthly government that rests on the shoulders of God. We then will continue our process of the restoration of all things with Christ seated on the throne of Israel.

In this time, we will experience an accelerated growth of righteousness and heavenly resources soaking into the land. Relationships that reflect kingdom life and produce heavenly atmospheres will shine. This is when the majority of the earth will really start looking and feeling like heaven. Many who have sowed into the earth with righteousness before Christ's return will continue to develop the land or the skill they labored in and also be assigned to various tasks that have to do with reigning with Christ: "if we endure, we will also reign with him" (2 Timothy 2:12).

In this time, we will be able to bring the glory of God developed in our lives before the Lord. "The Lord God Almighty and the Lamb are the city's temple. The city does not need the sun or the moon to shine on it, because the glory of God is its light, and the Lamb is the city's lamp. By its light the people of the world will walk and the <u>kings</u> <u>of the earth will bring their glory into it</u>" (Rev 21:22-24).

Each person will bring a different facet of God's nature and excellence as they display the very glory by which their unique relationship with Christ on earth produced. The excellence of the nature of God manifest in each one will come before Him freely. This will bring great joy to Jesus' heart as He sees the diverse manifestations of himself and unique displays of glory through each individual. This will be a partial fulfillment of the promise the Father made to Him that He would inherit the nations.

I love the story of Jesus in John chapter two. In this chapter Jesus does His first miracle and it says, "He thus revealed His glory" (John 2:11 BSB). This says a lot when studying the topic of God's glory. What this tells me is that the revealing of God's glory has to do with making something that's ordinary extraordinary. As Jesus pours out the quality of His new wine at the end of the age the quality of His people will acclimate. He is coming back for a bride without spot or wrinkle.

When I met my wife we had many supernatural experiences when getting to know one another. In the first week of us talking God was manifesting His presence in such a strong tangible way in both of our lives. We both were experiencing the same measure of the presence of God and hearing the same things at the same time. My wife received the revelation that this is one interpretation of what equally yoked means.

Before Christ returns the Father is going to begin to do this between the bride and the bridegroom so that His Son will have an equally yoked companion. The church will be in a place of receiving the same measure of presence that's on Jesus now. In order for this to happen the Father is going to draw the church into a whole new level of maturity and intimacy with himself.

Chapter Thirteen

THE DAWN OF A NEW DAY

And we all, with unveiled face, beholding the glory of the Lord, are

being transformed into the same image from one degree of glory to

another. For this comes from the Lord who is the Spirit.

2 Corinthians 3:18

Revelation 21:1 says, "Then I saw a new heaven and a new earth. The former heaven and the former earth had passed away." The phrase "passed away" in this verse is two English words that translate one Greek word. The Greek word they are translating is the word *aperchomai*. The meaning of this word is to separate a part from the whole. In other words, God is going to to separate and consume the parts of earth corrupted by wickedness and cloth the void with new life.

There is a concept in scripture that talks about forgetting the past and embracing the future. This concept is developed even further as we look into the end of the age. Isaiah prophesied of a time where we will no longer remember the lower level of living and the darkness of this age. "For behold, I create new heavens and a new earth; And the former things will not be remembered or come to mind." (Isaiah 65:17).

God wants our minds to be so enveloped with His glory that we are no longer affected or even remember the darkness of yesterday. "You will forget the shame of your youth and remember no more the reproach of your widowhood" (Isaiah 54:4). The glory of God will so overshadow every lesser thing.

As we get acclimated to God's glory His fire will burn away every lie from the Devil and every memory that doesn't line up with His love. As we progress from glory to glory His love will wash away the imprints, scars, and trauma left on the sands of our past, leaving us new ground to walk on in the innocence of our identities in Christ. God will remove the scars of our old man and give us new life in Him.

Paul pointed us to the right perspective when he said, "Set your minds on things above," and "whatever is true, whatever is noble, whatever is right, whatever is pure, whatever is lovely, whatever is admirable––if anything is excellent or praiseworthy––think about such things" (Colossians 3:2; Philippians 4:8, BSB). These scriptures give us a lens through which to view life that more accurately depict where we are headed as a human race. The word "renew" in Romans 12:2 means "to renovate." Renewing our minds is about removing the old and replacing it with the new.

Imagine yourself removing old furniture in your house to bring in the new. The old furniture represents painful memories from a sinful and sick world. God is removing and renovating those thoughts and bringing in atmospheres of "righteousness, peace, and joy in the Holy Spirit" (Romans 14:17).

We are at the brink of a new day for man-kind. There is something about watching the sunrise that captivates the soul. As the glow of the sun begins to envelope every corner, shadows begin to flee. Memories of the darkness begin to fade as the warmth and light of the sun clothe the earth. Soon enough the light brings out all the beautiful colors of God's creation.

There is a sunrise coming for us. We are about to enter into the age to come. Soon enough we will be standing on the new earth in resurrected bodies enveloped in the glory of God.

The good news is that we don't have to wait for Christ to come back to walk in His glory! We can bring God's glory into every area God assigns to us right now. We can even develop more of what we will be in the age to come by stewarding the gifts, skills, and responsibilities that God gives us. All of this can all be carried with us into the "world without end" (Ephesians 3:21 KJV).

The story of Paul teaches us how to shift atmospheres for kingdom advancement. He taught us to stand firm in our identities and flow with the Father. This lifestyle of revival will bring about a change in this earth leading up to the second coming.

As our thoughts align with Heaven, atmospheres will shift in our body, soul, and spirit along with the spaces around us. The knowledge of the glory of God will cover the earth as the waters cover the sea. "But thanks be to God, who always leads us in triumph in Christ, and manifests through us the sweet aroma of the knowledge of Him in every place" (2 Corinthians 2:14).

We will usher in the restoration of all things with Jesus as the head of the church. Jesus commissioned us to disciple nations. I believe there will be entire nations given over to the Lordship of Jesus Christ before the second coming. Entire nations will be preserved into the age to come. There will be cities and families that shine as lights to the world around them.

What happened with Paul in Ephesus is a small example of what will take place on a massive scale at the end of the age. The glory will flow from the Church causing the created order to respond. "The creation itself also will be set free from its slavery to corruption into the freedom of the glory of the children of God" (Romans 8:21).

Will you answer the call to be a glory carrier? Will you say "yes" to a relationship with the Bridegroom who has eyes of fire for you? Step into your God-given DNA and manifest as a son of glory!

THE DAWN OF A NEW DAY

NOTES

NOTES

50449110R00046

Made in the USA
Middletown, DE
25 June 2019